THE RHYTHM OF LIFE:

NONFICTION POETRY

THE RHYTHM OF LIFE:

NONFICTION POETRY

Large Print Edition

Karen J. Chism

Heartspeak Publications Incorporated
heartspeakpublications@gmail.com

THE RHYTHM OF LIFE:
NONFICTION POETRY
~*~

Copyright © 2014 by Karen J. Chism

Published by Heartspeak Publications
Incorporated, Michigan, USA

Unless otherwise noted, any references to: The Holy Bible, The Bible, or God's Word, refer to direct quotes or the author's paraphrasing of scripture from THE HOLY BIBLE, *KING JAMES VERSION.*

Cover Image – Copyright © HuHu/Shutterstock.com

Acknowledgements

After having published my first three books of poetry, I now appreciate all the hours of work that goes into getting a book ready to publish. My daughter, (Editor in Chief) and I are clearly astounded at how many times we *both* had overlooked the very *same* word—even after publication!

Editing my own writing quickly becomes ineffective and eventually pretty much . . . well, like WORK!

Having traveled that unpleasant road with my first three books, once again my loving, capable, and very reliable daughter came to the rescue! Also, thanks to Brian and Denise for proofing my final draft.

My rhyming comes relatively easy; and with age and health limiting my engagement in physical pursuits, I consider myself blessed to have this gift. A never-ending supply of ideas from daily life and study of The Bible furnish me with topics for my *nonfiction* poetry.

Last, but not least, my loving dear husband Jim, so patient—he offers me encouragement every time I run a new effort by him!

Love Ya

I thank my God, through my Lord and Savior Jesus Christ, for the inspiration and the strength to express myself in rhymes.
My prayer, desire, and mission—may all I write bring honor and glory to Him.

✝

Preface

My writings may be crude to some, that's okay. They are a collection of the expressions of what is on my mind, in this—the latter time of my life.

My writings, especially the poems, come to me in thoughts that rhyme. I seem to be compelled, addicted if you will, to put my thoughts to paper and pen. I am most greatly affected after studying the Word of God. Some may say, *It is Divine Guidance,* who can know for sure?

The preponderance of subject matter is from my life experience, and observing others in my favorite pastime of people watching.

I have no formal writing instruction; therefore, I am sure I fracture all the modern rules for grammar and structure, but I look not to be approved of mankind, but rather pray that my humble attempts will please my Lord.

If He chooses to use any of my writing to bring a person closer to Him, I would be honored and blessed that my words glorified God and blessed another person.

I desire my writing to convey a truthful, relatable, meaningful, and easily understood message—not merely a collection of fancy words, to befuddle the mind; but to shine light on some hard subjects that I deem to be difficult contemporary issues. Solutions and answers, it's all there; we just need to look . . . in God's Word.

I humbly hope to be able to share with you select gleanings, many from my own life, in my style of rhymes.

Table of Contents

The Rhythm of Memories

Memories flood in with certain music that I hear
All the places I've been with my husband so dear

A tune that has a beat of a sexy West Coast Swing
Can't sit still; visions of our dancing it still brings

Those were the days; dancing four times a week
Gliding across the floor; mastering our technique

Memories can evoke—heart rhythm changes
Resulting with beats—in dangerous ranges

Human emotions have rhythms all their own
Fear steps up the tempo, in overdrive they're
thrown

Pleasant memories bring calmness to my mind
The glorious sunrise; leaving darkness behind

Every stage of my life has its own cadence I find
Waltzing is slower, but more intimate; as
designed

The memory has a unique way of display
Surprising me sometimes like a grand buffet

2 | The Rhythm of Life

Angry staccato perhaps is better left behind
Not every recollection is welcome in my mind

Our day and our nights follow the tick of the clock
The sun hurries to plunge; darkness to unlock

Sometimes memories are all I have left
Illness has left me bereft

The forgotten ebb and flow of ordinary events
Awaken distant memories; unexpectedly present

<u>Memories</u>

Memories are made for someone, somewhere,
every minute of the day
Whatever we say or do, might be all that is left
for others to weigh

Memories are truly priceless; we can't buy, trade,
or change
There isn't a return department to beg and
exchange

Memories really are all that's of any lasting
measure
After we die; memories are what loved ones will
treasure

The material possessions we leave behind will
soon fade
Gold and silver doesn't count for much; for one
more day we'd gladly trade

The future can't make up for today's lost hours ill
spent
It matters little, if later we desire to repent

4 | The Rhythm of Life

Every day we must remind ourselves, as we go
about our life
We'll live on in *someone's* memory; praying their
recollections will be nice

<u>Self-Medicating</u>

Writing poetry is *self-medicating* in a way
Soothing action; forgetting woes of the day

Expressing myself with rhyming words
Enlarging thoughts; my method preferred

I suppose it is my opiate; compelling me to rhyme
Transporting me to a lovelier, more tranquil time

I can be uptight and stressed to the max
Reflecting in rhymes allows me to relax

This *habit* won't harm my body or soul
Bank account stays intact; family remains whole

Before my poem is complete, I drift toward God
His true peace releases my troubles; in Him I'm
awed

Karen J. Chism, 5/30/2014

<u>Our Love Story Began in 1954</u>

I remember with wonder, the day you picked me
Out of all my friends, in front of the diner, called
S&C

You boldly asked with teenage arrogance, "Will
you be my baby?"
I took one look at your *killer smile*, without any
caution I said, "Maybe"

You draped your arm around me with a
possessive air
This was just the beginning, of a lifelong love
affair

If I would have been older, I expect I might have
been afraid
A complete stranger laying hands on me, I should
dissuade

But several of my girlfriends were with me, at the
time
A young giddy teenager—I was flattered, he
chose me from the line

It wasn't *puppy love*; it was the real thing, never
to be forgotten
Though life events separated us; with the war
and other things rotten

Fast forward to 1984

Thirty years later, I remembered that special time
Everyone has a tale, just not like yours and mine

When meeting after all those years, we still had
something unique
This time however; you used a new technique

You introduced me to the love of Jesus Christ and
included Him in our union
That was the beginning of our blessed reunion

Proceed to the present - 2014

Fast forward now to 2014 and old age is upon us
Sixty years later; living for Christ has been a plus

The exciting rhythm when my heart skips a beat
With your loving smile that's still so sweet

The wondrous thing, is you still choose me above all
That kind of love can be expected, when you answer God's call

Was it just the act of an arrogant teenage boy?
I like to think God had some angels in His employ

<u>The First Couple</u>

The first man was Adam and his helpmate was
named Eve
They were disobedient, so out of the
garden—God made them leave

They didn't have much to worry about packing
Their clothes consisted of leaves, and shoes they
were lacking

But the weather was perfect; of this you can be
sure
Don't you envy them, when a snowy day we
endure?

I may be taking some literary license with the
detail
But I'm sure of one fact—they were male and
female

If that was not a fact, where would we come
from?
God had a plan; nobody could say He was dumb

From Adam and Eve all humans are related
Disobedience was in them, before they mated

I wonder if Adam and Eve got along or did they
fight
Probably they didn't know how to get it right

How could I imagine that, you may ask?
They disobeyed God; they were not up to the
task

If *they* couldn't figure it out, however can we?
We have the instructions written down you see!

But they had God talking directly to them
That doesn't mean they *listened* to The Great I
Am

As a loving couple, starting out with kisses
We tied the knot, made it Mr. and Mrs.

But that was only a beginning of living side-by-
side
Trouble around the corner, if our pride we didn't
hide

Ever wonder how something so beautiful *might*
turn to crap?
Slowly but surely all the plans *could* unwrap

I once remarked, "If you hurt my Jim, you hurt
me"
They laughed and mocked, not
understanding—he is one with me

God didn't throw only Eve from the garden
Adam had to go also; he didn't get a pardon

Eve was created from Adam's rib
They were intended together to live

Some can't comprehend, the hurt isn't separate
If it happens to one, the other it does devastate

There is a fix for the pain and grief you will find
If you do it *God's way*, and become of *one mind*

Don't follow the pattern of Adam and Eve
Therein, lies a lifetime of trouble, you'll grieve

After We Get Married

Have you ever reasoned . . .

—After we get married, things will change you'll see
—I always figured a change in our status; marital bliss it would be

—A change in my new spouse's behavior; the ring will make
That's assuming the union wasn't a fake

—A fake . . . I have the marriage license right here!
—We had the party and said our vows, witnessed by everyone dear

—We held the ceremony in a church this time
—So, unlike our first marriage, things will work out fine

—We lived together for two years to iron out all the kinks
—We are *in **love*** and don't care what anyone thinks
—Hush up; your negativity will bring us a jinx

*Did you go to a church thinking the Pastor's
blessing was all you needed?
You may have sought counsel from professionals
and their advice you heeded*

*—We have the same friends and respect each
other's space
—I understand the need of his ambitions and I
even embrace*

*You sure make a lovely couple and I get what
you're saying
I just want you to be sure, in the end you're not
paying
It is not a pretty picture I am portraying*

*The union of marriage is not just a tradition
Or your spouse an adornment to your life—an
addition*

*It is a man and a woman becoming "**one**," with
mutual submission
I haven't heard you mention God in your plans;
was that a conscious omission?*

I often hear people exclaim, "It's all good!"
Whose standard are you using; what would you
change if you could?

What things do you believe will change after you
tie the knot?
—Oh, that's negative thinking; out of my mind I
will blot

—We'll be fine, as long as we respect each
other's space
—That will be much easier when we get a larger
place

—A night out with the boys will help us stay
connected
—My need for my girlfriends, he has always
respected

But aren't you getting married to be with each
other?
—Yeah . . . but too much togetherness; love it
will smother

—I've heard that familiarity breeds contempt
But that unwanted state, marriage should
exempt

*You make the union so you can be closer in **all** ways*
If you like each other you will want to spend all your days

You expected all problems would improve after you tied the knot
Sadly, heartache may be all that you wrought

If you don't have important things in common, soon you will desire
Companionship with another—you will want to acquire

All of the hurdles you thought marriage would fix
Might become larger, if you leave God out of the mix

That Awful "S" Word

That awful "S" word, do you know the one I mean?
—Yeah, you're talking about sex, but it's in the gene

That's not the "S" word I'm talking about
—More dreaded then that, I don't doubt

Not even sin is as fearful as this word
—Well, tell me quick, what have you heard?

It's the one that Christian guys like to quote
Some men try to control you, they even may gloat

The gals all resist with a fierce battle cry
—Yah . . . it's easy for you, you have a good guy

It was not my idea at all you know
—Tell me quick or better yet, show

It has been around forever it seems
—You sure you're not reaching for extremes?

Wasn't it written down once and for all?
—Are you talking about Man's fall?

Yeah, now you're on the right track
—But all of my self-help books I would have to take back

Let's take a look in "The Book," it's near the back
There is a chapter to assure your relationship will remain on track

SUBMISSION— *is the word; "Yuck!" I can hear you now*
—But that won't work with us, unless you tell me how

Remember it is not my instructions, but straight from God's Word
Find it in Ephesians Chapter 5—for you to read, is preferred

It just works; **Wisdom from the Master's Mind**

Equally Yoked

The Apostle Paul warns us to be *equally* yoked
The *same* destination needs to be the goal
A team pulling a load working *together* is hoped
Avoiding a wreck; the *same* driver in control

God The Father is residing in Heaven above
Darkness can't have communion with light
Choosing a partner with **different** beliefs; to love
Slim chance of making that union right

Hanging with unbelievers; God will not dwell
Need to be *like minded* to expect spiritual growth
Accept His Son Jesus Christ; or be destined to Hell
For God desires to be the Father to us both

The Holy Spirit must give us the **same** instruction
Not a mind of our own, pulling a different way
An ox and a donkey; doomed to destruction
The best laid plans will helplessly go astray

We may find we're at odds with our chosen one
A marriage counselor, we may look to for a fix
Not as happy together as when we first begun
The Holy Bible has the best bag of tricks

Christ will guide us; so we won't go forth blind
Our union will be full of lasting pleasure
The Lord wants us to be together with *one mind*
Not pulling in different directions is the real
treasure

Karen J. Chism, 6/1/2014

~*~

The Lord instructs us in 2nd Corinthians 6:14, *King James Version* - "Be ye not unequally yoked together with unbelievers: for what fellowship hath righteousness with unrighteousness? And what communion hath light with darkness?"

After The Honeymoon

When you first fall in love and everything is new
You see nary a fault, or very few
No one else is important, but the two of you

When necessity causes you to be apart
Without your loved one there is a hole in your
heart
You can hardly wait for your next meeting to
start

The excitement rivals Christmas and birthdays
rolled into one
All other activities you reject, as no longer fun
Your time spent together, you enjoy a re-run

Little imperfections you minimize, even ignore
Surely only blissful happiness will be in store
It matters not that you heard he does snore

The heat and sparkle of the honeymoon will fade
Everyday life will interfere—when the bills need
to be paid
You may think; I never noticed *that*, I've been
betrayed

Nay, it isn't so, you just *see* with different feelings
Reality sets in and you have to start dealing
Pleading to God, as you are kneeling

Starting out with chemistry and sparks, but not
much respect
Ignoring God's guidance, upon this error you'll
reflect
Afraid the serious subject, your spouse may
reject

Is it too late for a do-over, what is it you want to
achieve?
You need to discover; what does the other
believe?
How can you recover this late, the love you
perceived?

When starting out, only the two of you mattered
Now all your dreams and hopes have been
shattered
Maybe you should have included God, and then
all wouldn't be tattered

22 | The Rhythm of Life

I speak of three in the relationship—that's best
The Lord Jesus is the honored guest
Including Him in everything assures a harmonious
nest

<u>Threefold Cord</u>

The divorce rate today gives testimony to the
failure of doing it *our way*
Doesn't seem to matter how grand the wedding
party or how much we pay

Maybe we think if we get married in a church
God will bless our life
We hope this act will protect us from all the strife

If we want God's blessing maybe it would be wise
To check out what rules for marriage, He has
devised

He left us a very large *Instruction Book*
Heartbreaking—there are those that never give it
a look

Oft-times couples marry with definite ideas of
their own
It is not long before realizing their plan is blown

The problem may be one spouse had a different
image of how it would be
Neither of them considered their union needed
three

Neither wanted to change their life or separate
from their mother
Their friends were too important to give up for
the other

They loved their new mate; that was not the
thing
But they wanted their spouse as an *addition*, like
new bling

To leave out of the union, The Author of marriage
in the first place
Increasing odds against their success; rather
insuring disgrace

The preacher proclaimed, "Let no man put
asunder"
How could this have happened; their marriage
vows trampled under?

They held the ceremony in a church—wanting a
good outcome
They legally *tied the knot*, in front of everyone

The knot they tied only consisted of the two
They are now up a creek in a paddle-less canoe

The world will toss them to and fro with its
advice
But, The Word of The One they hoped would
approve, is very concise

Yet, the answer they continue to look for in the
marriage classes
The same place that produced the failures of the
masses

It is all very simple, and will only cost them
prayerful time
God has higher credentials to fix their problems
they'll find

Make sure The Creator is at the center of the
knot you tied
He is ready, willing, and able to be your guide

~*~

Ecclesiastes 4:12 - "and if one prevail against him,
two shall withstand him; and a threefold cord is
not quickly broke"

Make Everyone Happy

Our desire is to just make everyone *happy*
Doesn't seem to work; it still turns out crappy

Oh, whatever are we doing wrong, can't seem to
get it right?
As a child of God we sometimes forget, many
have not seen "The Light"
In this world does abide, many *children of the
night*

Remembering that The Word of God does
proclaim
Darkness does hate The Light; and God's Word
they defame

A quote by an unknown author, seen on a church
marquee; points out a tragic flaw
If a child of God marries a child of the devil; he'll
always have trouble with his father in-law

God tells us in His Word, not to be yoked with an
unbeliever
The divorce rate lays testament to *the great
deceiver*

If, indeed we believe in The Creator who has a
plan
Why would we want to do anything other than?

If, we truly desire to get it right
We'd give up trying by our own might
And follow the instructions of **The Father of Light**

First, to our Creator we must have submission
There is that "S" word again—expressed an
admonition

Then, to one another we need to submit, the
order is our spouse after God
Next, consideration for our offspring; to change
positions would be flawed

Remember in the beginning, God created Adam
and then Eve
He told Adam to become one with his wife; and
to her he was to cleave

Some get it wrong and can't leave their father or
mother
Or even worse . . . cleave onto their children
instead of each other

To **make everyone happy** would mean wanting to please Satan
Perhaps for genuine happiness, priorities we need to straighten

If children are allowed to come between a husband and wife
Each are guaranteed a long life—of strife

If you are a Christian reading this rhyme
You will know where to get your instructions every time

When you do it God's way it will just work; my way turned out all wrong
It would behoove you to make sure to whose family you belong

I Was Thinking

The look of sheer panic in my husband's eyes
Whenever I say, "You know; I was thinking . . ."
We've been together long enough; he is wise
I glance in his direction as his heart is sinking

He *knows* my idea will entail money or work
Also, wise enough not to object or complain
Good husband that he is; his duty he won't shirk
He holds his breath; waiting for me to explain

"If we moved this over there and that over here
Those awful views; which are the first look
Would not be seen by all; it would just disappear
I saw this great idea in a new book"

I venture it's a scene played out the world wide
She has an idea . . . he replies, "Whatever you say"
I've seen this same look in his eyes since I was a bride
Best for him to agree at the start; he won't win anyway

Karen J. Chism, 6/1/2014, for Kris and Brian

Dancin'

Ballroom dancing with the love of my life for
years
Brings fond memories but also a measure of tears

Oh, how I loved to dress up just like when a little
girl
Put on a fancy skirt, showing off a bit of leg as I
twirl

Jim meticulously attired; so handsome—Fred
Astaire had nothing on him
We waltzed and we did the cha-cha as the lights
grew dim

We were in our 60's when we started the sport
We danced somewhere, four times a week; the
time *still too* short

We planned to attend many tea dances when we
retired
We continued our professional lessons as desired

All the fine clothes and dancing shoes, I now gave
away
Some other lady may be wearing, with her hips in
a sway

Health issues prevented our planned direction
We gave away all of our dance tape collection

It was so much fun; I don't regret all the monies
required
Ballroom dancing was good exercise and
closeness it inspired

Retirement

My first thought this morning, as I awakened from sleep
I wondered what time it was, at the clock I took a peek

Well, I can get up if I want, or roll over for a short snooze
But the splendid thing is, I was free to choose

I never needed an alarm to pull me out of bed
My internal clock worked better, instead

My first conscious thought as I stretched and planned out my day
I looked forward to the time I would spend learning of God's way

I made Bible reading a priority to start the morning
I knew it would set the tone for peace, even if it was storming

I didn't have a job or boss to dictate my
responsibilities
Free from those restraints balanced out any
disabilities

I could concentrate my energies upon pleasing
my Lord
In days gone by, thoughts of Him might have
been ignored

Thanks to The Father for the blessing of this
retirement time
Thankful for the motivation to express His ways,
in rhyme

These verses would never have been part of my
days while employed
Worldly pursuits would have taken precedence;
rhyming thoughts destroyed

Growing older is full of hidden blessings I've
found, arriving at this place
Didn't plan for times like these, while in the rat
race

Retirement is full of unexpected perks and
treasure
I'm looking forward to leisure and pleasure

If only my life can be a small testimony of God's
Grace
Oh, how I look forward to His dear embrace

**As the song proclaims; "It will be worth it all
when we see Jesus"**

✝

"It Will be Worth it All When We See Jesus" – by Esther K. Rusthoi

<u>Trust Your Heart?</u>

Belief in our heart is indeed an important thing
We believe in our heart, for salvation it will bring

In what and whom we place our trust is the key
Our own heart *can* deceive us, as we'll see

Every one may have a different or no god at all in mind
Self oft-times will be on the throne, as we will find

This would have disastrous results we are told
Rather than if we use the Bible for our mold

Trusting in self is **worse** than trusting in a man
Or any other god; **our own heart is worse** than

Thinking our heart will steer us right
The Bible says; isn't awfully bright

Besides not being wise; God said that it's **worse**
Than worshiping false gods—and God is adverse

To walk after the imagination of our evil heart
Worse than after other gods; if we don't depart

How is it that the very **best** thing that *men* advise?
Is the very thing that our God does despise?

Our heart *can*, and often does lead us astray
Thankfully, our God tells us of a better way

Karen J. Chism, 7/20/2014

~*~

Jeremiah the prophet answering the question;
"What is our sin that we have committed against the Lord our God?"

Jeremiah 16:12 - "And ye have done **worse than your fathers;** for, behold, **ye walk every one after the imagination of his evil heart,** that they may not hearken unto me:"

Again in Jeremiah 17:9 - "The heart is deceitful above all things, and desperately wicked: who can know it?"

<u>Unspeakable Grief</u>

Have you ever been so troubled that you could
not speak?
Has your grief ever been so strong that it made
you weak?

Has your mind ever been in a condition where
you couldn't think?
Have you ever shed so many tears your eyes
couldn't blink?

Have you ever faced a problem with no end in
sight?
Have you ever been so weary you wanted to give
up the fight?

Have you ever not even known what you should
pray for?
Your elbows on the bed, your bent knees on the
floor?

Only out of your mouth came a pathetic groan
The Holy Spirit makes intersession to the throne

He knows what we need according to the Will of
God
Even if we don't have a clue, we know His Will is
not flawed

He knows our heart and can see our need
Even if we don't know how to plead

Do you believe He is Sovereign; and this is His
Will concerning you?
Have you ever considered perhaps this is where
God wants you?

Surely, I don't have the answer to *your* personal
pain
In hard times, I grew closer to The Lord; that was
my gain

Karen J. Chism, 7/1/2014

~*~

Romans 8:26 - "Likewise the Spirit also helpeth
our infirmities: for we know not what we should
pray for as we ought: but the Spirit Itself maketh
intercession for us with groanings which cannot
be uttered."

<u>One Foot in & One Foot Out</u>

Put your right foot in and your right foot out
Could refer to a simple dance ditty to shout
Do the **Hokey Pokey**, and turn all about
Or **Hocus Pocus**; magic tricks bringing in doubt

Then again; one foot in the world and one in
Godly pursuits will produce
Mixed up, confused, unhappy persons; Satan to
seduce

A troubled evil person you may even know
Getting their impetus from love of the dough
Yet instruction from above; peace it will bestow

Karen J. Chism, 6/3/2014

~*~

James 1:8 - "A double minded man is unstable in
all his ways,"

James 3:16-4:1 - "For where envying and strife is,
there is confusion and every evil work."

James 3:18 - "And the fruit of righteousness is
sown in peace of them that make peace."

<u>Growing Old Isn't for Wimps</u>

Growing old is not for wimps
I used to walk five miles without any limps

They say, "It is all downhill after fifty"
Downhill **should** be easier; that would be nifty

Going uphill takes more strength and energy I
know
Now, my expectations have evaporated like the
snow

Downhill is not measured by a person's age
Health is more accurate to use for a gauge

I admit my boobs no longer lead the way as I go
They are in danger of being caught in my pants,
ya know

My chin seems to hide somewhere between my
neck and my chest
I can't say for sure, it was there when I dressed

Some issues cannot be avoided, nor controlled
Age plus health; can't thwart God's plan foretold

Life's road may deal me really rough bumps
Time to brace up; over rough places I jump

Can't give in or let the pain win
Do the best I can; try to face it with a grin

Karen J. Chism 5/13/2014

Dependables for the Brain

More often, when I ask my daughter a question these days
She will answer with this reoccurring phrase

"I **told** you"— this, that, or the other
Growing more impatient with her mother

I understand her frustration; my mom was ninety-nine
It too, was a frequent answer of mine

I know when we're older the brain doesn't keep
Something needs to be done for the frequent leak

If we put our heads together maybe we can invent
Adult diapers or the like, for the brain—you get my intent

Elders would line up at the neighborhood store
The establishments would need to stock even more

5/14/2014 by just me . . . (forgot name)

The Lord is Able

Why don't you believe The Lord turned the river into blood?
Or that God caused it to rain until there was a great flood?

—All of the stories in the Bible can't be true, (*you say*)
—Turn a rod into a serpent? No way!

—The plague of frogs is a fairy tale for sure
—If Jesus died, can anyone expect a cure?

—When I hear a donkey talking to me
Maybe then I'll reconsider, and bow down my knee

—Until then—I need proof and not just a book
—Men made up those stories and your money they took

Well, the Bible does say that God hardens some people's heart
He knew who those people would be right from the start

Indeed, He has chosen me to believe in His Word
When there are many others that only find it
absurd

This blinding to the truth, I read, was part of His
plan
Who am I to question the ways of the Great I Am?

Many will remark that if they were God, they
would eliminate pain
Abel would never have died by the hand of his
brother Cain

—If I was a god—there would be a whole
different set of rules
Some are so stubborn, God calls them fools

We whom are chosen to have faith even though
we have not seen
Will read the Words in His Book and the Truth we
will glean

Even though there are some that may never
believe
If this be God's Will, I may grieve
But, never the less to His Word I will cleave

~*~

Hebrews 11:1 - "Now faith is the substance of things hoped for, the evidence of things not seen."

Enter or Delete

Social media is *The Buzz* today
Leading our youth to moral decay
Giving boldness over to foul play
Kindness and manners are now passé

Hiding behind a computer screen
Isn't limited to the teen
Grandmas are incredibly mean
They are indeed the bully queen

Social media is not just for the young
It is home for those with a filthy tongue
Hiding behind *free speech*, spreading dung
Vile words right and left they have flung

Whenever one learns to use the keyboard
'Delete' as well as 'Enter' should be explored
Once you have hit the 'Enter' or 'Record'
Someone, somewhere knows how to restore

Social media makes it easy for hearts to break
Personalities and faces are routinely fake
You won't get a second chance or a retake
Your whole future might be at stake

Be very careful when you twitter or tweet
It takes as much thought to be nasty as sweet
Someday the very one you cursed, you may meet
Maybe you will want to consider the 'Delete'

We've all heard of cases where someone is dead
All because of something, a cowardly bully said
This type of behavior is disgustingly widespread
When on the internet, your words you can't
shred

In days of old, you were told to *take it outside*
Ugliness was hidden, a matter to deride
Texting has made easy — the anonymity and its
evil to hide
Do you even know where the delete key resides?

Better to leave the garbage unsaid
Than finding you can't delete or shred

<u>The Blame Game; So Lame</u>

The *Blame Game*; I discouraged years ago
Responsibility; hoping my children will grow

A childhood excuse when wanting to escape
Hoping the circumstances, to reshape

Doesn't wash with me; so and so did this and that
Perhaps it's the action, we need to combat

But the past is just that; what is happening *now*?
Will you be able to make it better; if so, how?

If wrong should be amended, don't look back
What will *you* do *today*, that history can track?

Light on others' faults, won't cover *your* sin
Regardless of how inventive, you make the spin

Proclaiming a situation should be accepted today
Won't change something wrong, or make it okay

Because *someone else* did far worse in your eyes
Doesn't justify, or make *you* look wise

What's more, it just plain doesn't work
Maybe your responsibility, you just want to shirk

Didn't fly with God, when Adam blamed Eve
Adam was an accomplice; The Lord it did grieve

Not seeking the facts, trusting your peers' review
You really think another's error, will excuse you?

You alone are responsible for your actions
Even though it may be a temporary distraction

Attention to another's faults; yours it won't hide
Another's guilt; won't brush yours aside

If you deem a situation, should be modified
Blaming the past, just keeps you preoccupied

It will only make you look a little deranged
And your situation will not be changed

Ranting and raving about others' misdeeds
Does nothing for the solution, or how to proceed

When the need arises, to defend your deed
Blaming another's faults, won't help you succeed

Do you automatically want to run and hide?
When you know in your heart it is only pride?

To grumble and gripe, about the left- or right-wing
It never altered any person, place, or thing

The *Blame Game*, *truly* is so lame
The energy wasted is a downright shame

Karen J. Chism, 7/11/2014

<u>Wisdom</u>

Wisdom will come to all those who seek
Those who think they know it all, only get a peek

God tells us wisdom is more precious than gold
Choose wisdom over getting rich; we are told

Understanding is right up there on the Master's
list
With knowledge not far behind; be sure they are
not missed

We won't find these jewels going down a wicked
path
At least not gems that we can hold on to, or that
last

Wisdom can be found in God's Word, we are
promised
This blessing will always be just out of reach for
the dishonest

Pride keeping them just short and always adrift
The foolish person is kept from this wondrous gift

The fear of the Lord is the beginning of the right
way
A good start is learning to get on our knees and
pray

Durable riches and righteousness we cannot put
in the bank
When we acquire the right stuff, The Lord we will
thank

Treasures that are gained from wickedness we
will regret
If we are too comfortable, The Lord we will forget

Wisdom, God tells us, is the thing to prize
Be sure your counselor speaks truth in God's eyes

God tells us that thoughts of the righteous are
right
The opposite of evil; their thoughts will indict

Counsels of the wicked are deceit; and we need
to discern
Careful from whom we ask advice, so that it is
truth we learn

We will gain a great defense—a measure of
protection
When we scour the pages of God's Word for
direction

Those that laugh at God's suggestions will prove
to be fools
Going through life never paying attention to His
rules

I can only say to those who think they have a
better way
Show me the world *you* have created this day

When man builds an automobile he includes an
instruction book
He would expect everyone to at least take a quick
look

Some try to navigate this world without a
plan—that is unwise
Every man doing whatever is right in his own eyes

That has always disappointed our Creator and
even brought out His wrath
Over and over we are cautioned, not to go down
that wicked path

Wisdom, understanding, and knowledge of the Lord's kind
These are better than all the worldly riches and pursuits of *our* mind

Karen J. Chism 7/4/2014

Big Mouths in High Places

Seems like, the higher up the ladder some go
The fuller of self they get; along with dough

When put on the spot, ya think they would know
Blaming your predecessor—is a big no-no

Some talk a good game, but don't have a clue
Excuses they made; promises not carried through

But a humble spirit didn't come with the job
Rather it produced, a bigger lynch mob

Appearances—in fancy clothes attempting to
hide
While denying a promise; their error amplified

The more on display, the greater chance to trip
Might be wiser to do less flapping of their lip

Whatever merit might be in what I proclaim
There will never cease, those thirsting for fame

Karen J. Chism, 7/12/2014

Up, Up, and Away

Most average people I've found
Say, "I'm not bad enough to be headed to Hell"
No thought to how they'll get out of the ground
Believing in Heaven they will dwell

Insisting they will go to Heaven when they die
They never seriously investigated their belief
It is more comfortable for them to believe a lie
Trying to explain what God says; gives them grief

I've asked them; "Do you have any *guarantee*?
Do you have a ticket, for *the* trip high in the sky?
Do you have a reservation, who is *your* trustee?
Shouldn't you have a plan, *before* you die?"

To rise up, once they are down
A feat they can't accomplish if they are dead
Through six feet of mud and dirt so brown
To get up and away, they'll need Christ, The Head

Karen J. Chism, 7/15/2014

Affixed to My Core

A morning shower with its calming ministrations
Loosens ancient doctrine affixed to foundations

Revelations—acquired from reading God's Word
Wash erroneous teachings from past-times heard

Rhymes flowed franticly from deep within my
core
Like the impurities I scrubbed away from my
pores

Expressing my thoughts these days in prime-time
Quickly connecting together; creating a rhyme

Typing on the keyboard; rhythmic and witty
Those with only foul words to express; I pity

Karen J. Chism, 6/3/2014

~*~

James 3:10 - "Out of the same mouth proceedeth
blessing and cursing. My brethren, these things
ought not so to be."

Meltdown

I pressed several tissues hard against my eyes
To force the tears back where they came from
Deep breaths preventing sobs turning to cries
Head throbbing and pounding like a base drum

Release of one tear; hard to hinder their flow
Like the gush of a fast moving stream
Not able to dam them up, immersed in my woe
Hand covering mouth—from the inevitable
scream

Talking is rendered an impossible task
Breathing is difficult; coming in short moans
Finally—remembering my Father in Heaven to
ask
For all the comfort for my heart and my bones

Going to my knees is the correct place to be
Changing my focus from trying on my own
Confident my Lord will hear my plea
He is not sleeping; He is on His Throne

Karen J. Chism, 5/28/2014

<u>News Regarding Cancer</u>

Heard on the news today
Advising physicians to say

You have a slow growing lesion
In this or that region

Not to use the word "Cancer," or bring fear
Patients wanting expensive treatment to clear

Makes me angry as all get out!
Who, but the doctors brought all the fear about?

I am talking from 18 years of experience I want
you to know
From the very first lump in my breast—what a
blow

The doctor begged me, to put in a port that day
He warned if I refused, with my life I would pay

Now—on my fourth Cancer, fighting every which
way
Poisoning, cutting, and throwing organs away

*Why **now** are they reversing their advice?*
You think it could have anything to do with price?

With all the insurance changes this year
Now it doesn't pay to instill patients with fear

Or maybe the plan is just to let people die
Bet we are just pawns for politicians on high?

This was on the news today 5/6/2014

Broken Heart Remedy

My heart was broken; gaping wide
A chasm so deep, none could fill
Only the Majesty of Christ should abide

When each new trauma comes into my life
Opening the break anew
More room for Christ to replace the strife

Turning a seemly bad thing to good
Not understanding at that moment
But, God knew that I soon would

Not asking for terrible things to upset my day
Yet, with His Grace, comes His comfort
Most everything just turns out okay

Truly, as the Scripture does proclaim
I can do all things through Christ
Who strengthens me; Him I will never defame

Maybe if all seems to be going our way
Our need wouldn't be as obvious
As it is when we have a really bad day

A broken heart can be the worst pain
Speaking of the heart that is connected to the brain
That can be fixed by calling on Jesus' name

Karen J. Chism, 5/12/2014

The Battle

I called upon Jesus my Lord
My cry did enter into His ears
Enemies too numerous to record
Trusting my Lord, dispelled all my fears

Hatred they flung my way
Fetching, luring, and despicable
Liars enticing foul play
Chasms eventually unfixable

Jealously smoldered without flame
Till opportunity of a tragedy
Allowed expression to defame
Plundering, stalking, and unified banditry

Pleasing one another rather then
Considering His eye watches all
Thwarting evil ends, Amen!
Against deceits, He erected a wall

Karen J. Chism, 5/21/2014

Veto Power of Duchess

Whatever Dad or I make plans to do
Duchess exercises her power over us two

Barely six pounds soaking wet is she
Dare not acknowledge her naïveté

Voicing her displeasure as we reach for our coat
Elevated to Master her position to promote

We put her in her pillow-top bed, where she
Humbly accepts her fate as we flee

When bedtime hour arrives, if we don't heed
She'll fuss and bark until we concede

She will grumble and pester us to no end
Why are they called man's best friend?

Oh, loyal she surely is, there's no denying that
But sometimes she acts the part of a brat

When visitors come into our home she will demand
Attention, kisses, or a pat from their hand

She will then settle down and intently watch
every move
Sweet little thing—until you get up to leave; then
she'll disprove

She will attempt to prevent you going to the door
Using her veto power from ten inches off the
floor

Like a sheep dog's nature, to herd all her charges
in sight
Duchess tries to keep all her people in one bunch,
nice and tight

She is as cute as can be—
This is no democracy—
Duchess has veto power you see!

But alas, her veto power does finally end
Can't make her own dinner; we're her best
friend!

Grace Squandered?

We are so blessed to live in the wondrous *Age of Grace*
Christ paid—with His precious *blood*—all our sins to erase

Now, forgiveness is granted for sinners like you and me
Repentance is expected of us though; you see

God our Heavenly Father has forgiven us, it is true
However; He expects some *changes* from me and you

If we go right out and commit the same act
What kind of repentance is that?

The Bible makes a distinction between *Godly sorrow*
And *sorrow of the world*; and what it will bring on the morrow

This is the *Age of Grace* we are quick to exclaim
Seems like squandering His precious Grace is a shame!

The Holy Bible says *Godly* sorrow worketh repentance to salvation
Worldly sorrow won't keep us from temptation

Even worse than that, the Bible claims worldly sorrow worketh death
These matters need to be considered before our last breath

Like my wee one that will tearfully cry; sorry am I
Will pain me if he is caught in another lie

The Bible says **not** to grieve The Holy Spirit of God
To squander His Grace makes our sorrow a fraud

Karen J. Chism, 5/17/2014

~*~

2 Corinthians 7:10 - "For godly sorrow worketh repentance to salvation not to be repented of: but the sorrow of the world worketh death."

Ephesians 4:30 - "And grieve not the Holy Spirit of God, whereby ye are sealed unto the day of redemption."

<u>Heaven Now or Later</u>

Got to musing this morning, as one tends to do
Resurrection life, is closer in view

Some believe, as soon as we draw our last breath
In Heaven we'll be immediately; after our death

That would mean, (like some believe) those that
previously died
Won't join with those on The Lord's Day;
gathered and resurrected worldwide

If up from the grave He will call us to meet
Will we need to *go back* to the grave before that
feat?

The Holy Bible speaks of the return of Jesus Christ
on a *certain day*
To gather all those that are His and take them
away

If we are already there—where will He take us?
What of the **Blessed Hope** of the Christian—what
than is all the fuss?

I know it doesn't bring much comfort to think of a
loved one in the ground
Just waiting for *the* special day when Christians
will *all* be Heaven bound

But while they are waiting for God's plan to be
carried out
They will not be aware of the passage of time; till
awakened to hear the trumpets' shout!

If I'm not face to face with Christ till "that day"
Fellowship will ensue; magnificently Gods way
I won't presume to modify God's plan; no way!

Heaven now or later—we can't have it **both** ways
The Bible proclaims at the last trump, us He will
raise

Karen J. Chism, 5/12/2014

~*~

1 Corinthians 15:52 - "In a moment, in the
twinkling of an eye, at the last trump: for the
trumpet shall sound, and the dead shall be raised
incorruptible, and we shall be changed."

<u>Go With the Flow</u>

"Go with the flow," expressed by those
An attitude some ignorantly chose

With nary a concern for right or wrong
Fellowshipping, singing the masses' song

Perhaps, like I told Mom as a kid
"Everybody's doing it; why forbid?"

If *everybody* jumped off the bridge,
Pray we would halt at the ridge

Common sense—Mom reasoned that day
Growth in The Lord showed a better way

The *flow* to me has a spiritual meaning
God's Sovereignty accepted; His intervening

His Flow I desire to go with; **His** Will be done
Blessed with all things from Holy Father and Son

That requires a profound walk with Christ
A privileged place I humbly take; He paid the
price

As time left on this earth necessarily shrinks
I welcome my Savior's call in a wink

Common sense from Mom may have saved me then
But knowledge of the Cross; now brings salvation, Amen!

Karen J. Chism, 5/12/2014

Can we know?

Can any mortal know for certain?
Evil or blessing, has God Omnipotent sent?
Limited vision, as behind a curtain
Heartbreaking events with His consent

Recorded passages in the Holy Bible
The Spirit-filled-pen of chosen men wrote
I dare not accuse them of libel
Nor willing to ignore—or—sugarcoat!

Troubling accounts of a loving God . . . killing all
Failing to obey Him; was the greatest sin
Accountable, every one large and small
Does He *now,* just turn His face for evil to win?

I know Christ paid for my sin on the cross
Or I would have died long ago
It surely is His prerogative; for He is Boss
He's not obligated to the status quo

God causing evil is hard to comprehend
Accepting the Sovereign's authority none the less
Worshiping other gods I don't recommend
Those thus engaged; He'll never bless

He does whatever He wills, He alone is just
Alive, omnipresent, not missing a thought
Whatever He does we must trust
Knowing this too, He has wrought

While an event is playing out, not to our liking
We _can know,_ He arranged; it's His plan
If He doesn't will it; He would be striking
My opinion doesn't get a vote, nor can I ban

Karen J. Chism, 5/12/2014

~*~

But . . . permit me to _paraphrase_ John 9:31 of
the Holy Bible: Now we do know this that God
does not hear sinners; but if any be a worshipper
of God, and doeth his will, Him He will **hear**. In
summary, He will hear, not necessarily do.

Easter Sunday

It is a breathtakingly beautiful Michigan day
Finally, all of the snow shovels are put away

I can't help but ponder on the Resurrection reminder for all
All those that are found in Christ Jesus when God makes *the* call

I just know it will be a glorious beginning; akin to spring
We'll fly up and away as on an angel's wing

I don't know if that is exactly how I will travel
But, then—all those mysteries, He will unravel

As the buds on the tree unfurl larger each warm day
My understanding will undoubtedly grow as the gentle breezes play

I don't envision any spring tornadoes or storms
Blue skies and sunny days—probably the norms

It actually stresses my brain to think of the
magnificent evermore
How can I possibly guess what God has in store?

If He made all the wonder of this very world in six
days
Oh, if that is from his inventory but a *sample* to
gaze

No wonder the Apostle Paul reported so little
detail
Or maybe his eyes could only see through a veil

I get so excited when I know God's promises are
nothing but true
I feel such sorrow for all those that only have a
worldly view

Their desires all concentrating on wealth, fun,
and games
In The Book of Life; won't be written their names

Some have boasted their belief; they will make
the most of **this** ride
They don't have a problem believing; forever in
the grave they'll reside

To believe in Jesus is a blessed gift not everyone
has received
For my loved ones that did not accept; I'll be
forever grieved

<u>April</u>

It's April 2nd and the first day nice enough for a walk
Still a bit chilly, but made it all the way round the block

Duchess was happy she could finally get some fresh air
She didn't need a coat, but I needed one to wear

The sun was shining brightly, the sky was so clear
It was wonderful to be outside without my snow gear

My love walked by my side, well actually two paces ahead
"Slow those long legs down a bit, honey," I pled

Under the large pine tree by my kitchen window, I saw
One tiny Crocus poking up through the dirt; hurrah!

I love this time of year when each day brings a new bud
Less of the dirty black over white snow and crud

I feel so blessed to live where the seasons change
Boredom can't set in when there is a constant
exchange

I know—the winter has been brutal some days,
around here
Just makes me more appreciative of spring and
fall, so dear

It won't be long I expect and we can complain of
the heat
But people from the south will visit here and find
it sweet

Silly humans, we are never satisfied for long
I would like days like these to linger and prolong

When we get older it's common for seniors to
complain
It gets more difficult to tolerate the changes yet
again

My Mom used to say she could tolerate the cold
better then the heat
At that time, I didn't agree with her as 80 degrees
couldn't be beat

I'd lie out in the sun till I burned to a crisp (like a fool)
The hotter the better for me was the rule

These days for me, I love the spring and the fall the best
Fortunate for Michiganders there are changes for all the rest

Karen J. Chism, 4/2/2014

<u>Weather</u>

It is really all about perspective
But sometimes that's only subjective

A Michigan day in early March, described as mild
The very same weather in June is considered wild

What is beautiful to one set of eyes that has viewed
Another may find not nice at all; they will conclude

A fresh landscape all crisp, clean, and white
Takes my breath away as I look on with delight

Some just look out the window with a heart of dread
Liking nothing about the cold, but instead

Some can't wait for the sunshine to give us the heat
These folks are happy with sweat running down their cheek

A perfect day for me is seventy-two
Others need eighty-five or they're blue

God had a plan for all kinds of weather; He said,
"It is good"
Yet the reason for tornadoes and hurricanes, I
never understood

Just because I don't like the weather, doesn't
mean God is not aware
God never promised me, all His plans He would
share

If for no other reason than a subject to talk about
Everyone will express an opinion, no doubt

The kids will shout with joy—another school
closing—time for play
Mom and dad wonder what they will do with the
kids today

Dad won't be happy on his drive to the shop
Or with all the ice on his windshield he has to
chop

If it is bad enough he can't get to work at all
The kids aren't aware of dad's paycheck, or how
small

So I perceive the weather does play a big part in
our mood
But I'm thankful we are all safe with this blessing
I'll conclude

Guns

There are many that would take away the **right** in
this country to *bear arms*
As if guns are the **only** means to use when
someone wants to do harm

This morning in the news is an account of a new
school *evil event*
Twenty people injured—as of this moment, not a
gun in sight, but a perpetrator hell bent

He used a *knife* to implement his dastardly deed
A gun is not needed to cause someone to bleed

Oh—that a few responsible law abiding persons
would have been around
But . . . it's ***a gun free zone***; licensed gun owners
can't be found

The *would be killer* is not harmed—we will spend
a lot of resources, but won't call the motive *sin*
Guaranteed the so-called *experts* will blame mom
or dad—in court he will win

Guess it is time to try banning fists and knives

~~~~~~~~~~

Thank you so much for reading this book. It has brought me joy to write, publish, and share the fourth collection of my poems.

If you are reading this page, I hope it means you enjoyed my rhyming enough to read to the end. If that is the case, I would be extremely honored if you would tell others by writing a review on the retailer's website where you purchased my book.

Additionally, I hope you will look for my other books:
—Reflections in My Twilight Years—Collection One
—Reflections in My Twilight Years—Collection Two
—Reflections in My Twilight Years—Collection Three

Thank you again and God bless,

Karen

<u>Editor's Note</u>

Although, Karen only arrived onto the writing scene this spring, she has already written her fourth book and is gaining a fan base for her poetry.

Excerpts from some internet reviews of her other books–

- ❖ Insightful
- ❖ . . . faith-filled . . .
- ❖ . . . deep emotion . . .
- ❖ I'm not usually a poetry fan, but this collection is great!
- ❖ Book was very enjoyable.
- ❖ I will be ordering the other two books soon.
- ❖ Shows great emotion, humor . . .
- ❖ I appreciate the author's creativity . . .
- ❖ Thought provoking elements to ponder in my own life.
- ❖ Shows intimate relationship she has with Jesus Christ.

I agree with the above reviews. I have enjoyed reading Karen's writings and hope to be involved in publishing many more of hers in the future. Karen often says, "Our lifestyle echoes our beliefs," and her rhymes illustrate this truth beautifully. I find her poems to be poignant, relevant, entertaining, wise, profound, and thought provoking.

I am convinced that you will enjoy this and her other books; finding your emotions stirred as you read about both age old and contemporary situations you can relate to and even learn from.

> — K. Compton, Editor in Chief, Heartspeak Publications Incorporated.

If you would like to receive updates concerning future offerings by Heartspeak Publications Incorporated or this author; ask to be added to our mailing list by sending an e-mail to:

heartspeakpublications@gmail.com

Heartspeak Publications Incorporated
Logo design by: K. Compton

www.ingramcontent.com/pod-product-compliance
Lightning Source LLC
Chambersburg PA
CBHW070539030426
42337CB00016B/2265